A New Tune A Day™ for Piano

Boston Music Company
part of the Music Sales Group
New York/Los Angeles/Nashville/London/Berlin/Copenhagen/Madrid/Paris/Sydney/Tokyo

Foreword

Since its appearance in the early 1930s, C. Paul Herfurth's original *A Tune A Day* series has become the most popular instrumental teaching method of all time. Countless music students have been set on their path by the clear, familiar, proven material, and the logical, sensibly-paced progression through the lessons within the book.

The teacher will find that the new books have been meticulously rewritten by experienced teachers: instrumental techniques and practices have been updated and the musical content has been completely overhauled.

The student will find clearly presented, uncluttered material, with familiar tunes and a gentle introduction to the theoretical aspects of music. The books are now accompanied by audio CDs of examples and backing tracks to help the student develop a sense of rhythm, intonation and performance at an early stage.

As in the original books, tests are given following every five lessons. Teachers are encouraged to present these as an opportunity to ensure that the student has a good overview of the information studied up to this point.

The following extract from the foreword to the original edition remains as true today as the day it was written:

The value of learning to count aloud from the very beginning cannot be over-estimated. Only in this way can a pupil sense rhythm. Rhythm, one of the most essential elements of music, and usually conspicuous by its absence in amateur ensemble playing, is emphasized throughout.

Eventual success in mastering the instrument depends on regular and careful application to its technical demands. Daily practice should not extend beyond the limits of the player's physical endurance — the aim should be the gradual development of tone control alongside assured finger-work.

Music-making is a lifelong pleasure, and at its heart is a solid understanding of the principles of sound production and music theory. These books are designed to accompany the student on these crucial first steps: the rewards for study and practice are immediate and lasting.

Welcome to the world of music!

A note to the teacher

While fingerings are provided for many exercises and pieces in this book, students are encouraged to investigate alternatives for themselves wherever possible. The danger of "playing by numbers" exists so long as comprehensive fingerings are offered, especially among the eager beginner. The teacher is urged therefore to nurture in the student a sense of curiosity and adventure, through which a keen and reliable instinct for sensible fingering can be developed. The ability to organize fingerings within the ranges of notes used in each piece is an essential skill for the serious pianist.

Published by
Boston Music Company

Exclusive Distributors:
Music Sales Corporation
257 Park Avenue South, New York, NY 10010, USA
Music Sales Limited
14-15 Berners Street, London W1T 3LJ, England
Music Sales Pty. Limited
120 Rothschild Avenue, Rosebery, Sydney, NSW 2018, Australia

This book © Copyright 2006 Boston Music Company,
A Division of Music Sales Corporation, New York

Edited by David Harrison
Music processed by Paul Ewers Music Design
Original compositions and arrangements by Moira Hayward
Cover and book designed by Chloë Alexander
Photography by Matthew Ward
Model: Tom Green
Printed in the United States of America
    by Vicks Lithograph and Printing Corporation
Backing tracks by Guy Dagul
CD performance by Moira Hayward
CD recorded, mixed and mastered by Jonas Persson and John Rose

Sincere thanks to the City Literary Institute, London, for their
invaluable help.

Your Guarantee of Quality
As publishers, we strive to produce every book to the highest commercial
standards. The music has been freshly engraved and the book has been
carefully designed to minimize awkward page turns and to make playing
from it a real pleasure. Throughout, the printing and binding have been
planned to ensure a sturdy, attractive publication which should give years
of enjoyment. If your copy fails to meet our high standards, please inform
us and we will gladly replace it.

www.musicsales.com

Contents

Rudiments of music

The staff

Music is written on a grid of five lines called a *staff*. Piano music is written on two *staves*.
At the beginning of each staff is placed a special symbol called a *clef* to describe the approximate range of the music.

This example shows a *treble clef* on the top staff, and a
bass clef on the bottom staff.
Music on the top staff is mainly played with the right hand,
and music on the bottom staff is mainly played with
the left hand.

The staff is divided into equal sections of time,
called *bars* or *measures*, by *barlines*.

Note values

Different symbols are used to show the time value of *notes*, and each *note value* has an equivalent symbol for a rest,
representing silence.

   The **eighth note**, often used to signify a half beat, is written with a
solid head and a stem with a tail. The eighth-note rest is also shown.

   The **quarter note**, often used to signify one beat, is written with a
solid head and a stem. The quarter-note rest is also shown.

   The **half note** is worth two quarter notes. It is written with a
hollow head and a stem. The half-note rest is placed on the middle line.

   The **whole note** is worth two half notes. It is written with a
hollow head. The whole-note rest hangs from the fourth line.

Other note values

Note values can be increased by half by adding a dot after
the notehead. Here a half note and a quarter note are together
worth a *dotted* half note.

Grouping eighth notes

Where two or more eighth notes follow each other, they can be
joined by a *beam* from stem to stem.

Time signatures

The number of beats in a bar is determined by the *time signature*, a pair of numbers placed after the clef.
The upper number shows how many beats each bar contains, while the lower number indicates what kind of note value
is used to represent a single beat. This lower number is a fraction of a whole note so that 4 represents quarter notes
and 8 represents eighth notes.

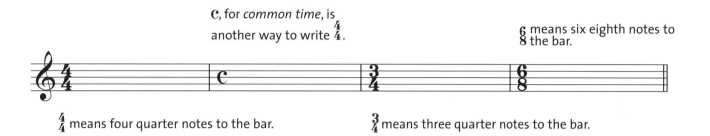

$\mathbf{C}$, for *common time*, is
another way to write $\frac{4}{4}$.

$\frac{6}{8}$ means six eighth notes to
the bar.

$\frac{4}{4}$ means four quarter notes to the bar. $\frac{3}{4}$ means three quarter notes to the bar.

Note names

Notes are named after the first seven letters of the alphabet and are written on lines or spaces on the staff,
according to pitch.

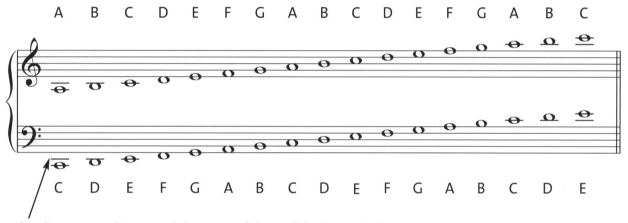

Ledger lines are used to extend the range of the staff for low or high notes.

Accidentals

The pitch of a note can be altered up or down a *semitone* by the use of sharp and flat symbols.
These temporary pitch changes are known as *accidentals*.

The *sharp* (♯) raises the pitch of a note.   The *natural* (♮) returns the note to its original pitch.

The *flat* (♭) lowers the pitch of a note.

Barlines

Various types of barlines are used:
Double barlines divide one section of music from another.   *Final* barlines show the end of a piece of music.

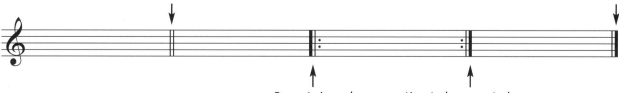

Repeat signs show a section to be repeated.

Before you play:

Buying or renting an instrument

• Electronic keyboards

If you have an electronic piano, safety is important. While there are built-in safety features on all new models, you can enhance these by using a circuit breaker every time the instrument is used. Avoid dangling cables, even if this means placing a rug over the cable, and ensure that the instrument sits squarely on its stand. For electronic pianos, headphones give the option of "silent" practice. Be aware, prolonged use of headphones at high volume can lead to hearing damage so be sure to monitor sound levels and ask your teacher's advice on a suitable pair.

Electronic pianos are more popular with some people because they tend to be more portable, need less maintenance and can offer facilities for practicing without disturbing neighbors.

The sound and feel of electronic pianos has improved greatly in recent years, but for many people there will never be any substitute for an acoustic instrument, either upright or grand.

Be sure to visit a reputable dealer and always take someone with you who knows something about these instruments, such as your teacher.

It is often possible to arrange for the rental of an instrument through a piano specialist.

• Piano Stools

It is very important to sit at the right height when playing and a proper stool, with height adjustment, is essential.

• Piano Tuners

You may find that a first tuning is included in the purchase price of your piano, but if not you should ensure the piano is tuned by a reputable tuner every so often. Many tuners recommend a tuning every six months, but some pianos prove to be very stable and therefore every nine months or even longer is adequate.

• Keys

• Piano stool

• Foot pedals

• Short Nails

Playing any kind of keyboard instrument is not compatible with long nails. They restrict freedom of optimum finger movement and can be painful if caught between the keys.

Practice

Playing any musical instrument is a combination of physical and mental agility, and these will both be developed with regular attention. Fun and long-term satisfaction rely on building a regular practice routine.

Golden rules for practice:

1. Make sure that each session has a variety of activities so you develop all-around skills and motivation.
2. With each new activity be clear about what you are aiming for. Ask your teacher if you are unsure.
3. Listen constantly to every sound you make—don't stop playing until you are pleased with your progress.
4. Establish a steady pulse in everything you play.

Posture

How and where you sit is important if you are to get the best sounds out of the piano and maximize the mobility of your ten fingers!

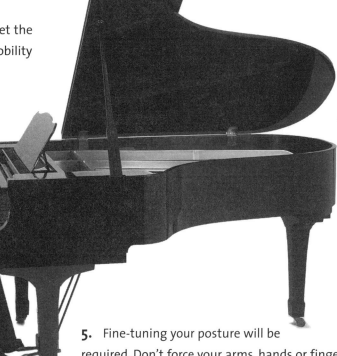

Don't force your arms, hands or fingers into a position that causes tension just in order to conform to a regulated position.

1. Sit towards the front of the stool and in the middle with your weight on your feet.

2. Sit up, but without tensing muscles or arching your back unnaturally.

3. Have the stool at a height that allows your forearms to be parallel with the backs of your hands—ask your teacher to show you.

4. The basic hand position needs to be relaxed with fingers gently curved, as though you are holding a softball that mustn't be squeezed too hard.

5. Fine-tuning your posture will be required. Don't force your arms, hands or fingers into a position that causes tension just in order to conform to a regulated position.

6. Regularly check that every part of your body feels free of tension and breathe easily as you play.

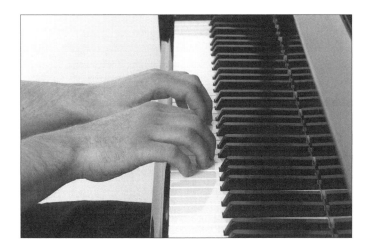

goals:

1. **The keyboard**
2. **Fingering**

3. **Half notes and quarter notes**
4. **Playing with a steady pulse**

The keyboard

All keyboards have the same layout. Notice how the groups of black keys alternate in twos and threes. Using this pattern, it's easy to identify the white notes.

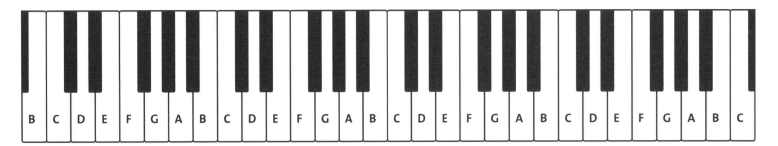

Using any finger on your right hand, play the white key that sits between the group of two black keys in the middle of the keyboard. This note is **D**.

Now moving your hand in a high arching movement, bounce lightly from one D to the next, moving up the piano.

Notice how the sounds get higher the further to the right you play.

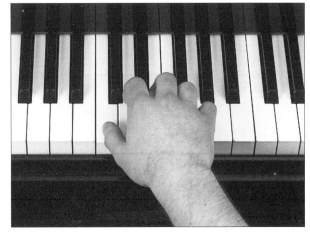

Now with your left hand, find the white key on the right-hand side of the group of three black keys closest to the middle of the keyboard. This note is **B**.

Using the same movement as before, play all the Bs and listen to the sounds getting lower as you go to the left.

Now play these notes from notation.
Quarter notes look like: ♩ and are worth a count of 1   Half notes look like: ♪ and are worth a count of 2

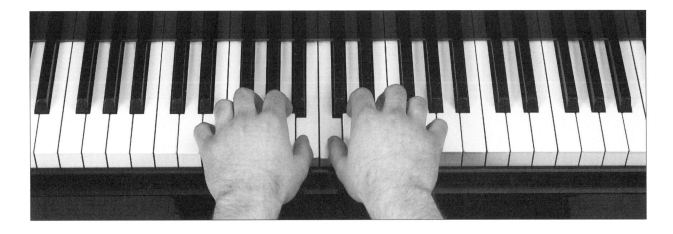

Exercise 1:

Count a steady pulse before you begin in order to set the speed and then count as you play to give the music basic stability.

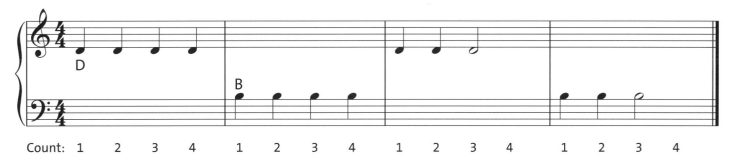

Count: 1 2 3 4   1 2 3 4   1 2 3 4   1 2 3 4

You can see from the diagram (left) that the keyboard is arranged in alphabetical order: if you move one white key to the right you'll move forwards through the alphabet from A to G, and moving one key to the left moves back a letter.

Activity

Find each of the seven letters. Try using different fingers, hands and positions on the keyboard, and remember to refer to the patterns of black keys to locate the white keys.

FINGERING

No one finger belongs exclusively to any one note on the piano, but it is really important to use fingers wisely, as there are so many possible keys.

In piano music the fingers of both hands are numbered thus:

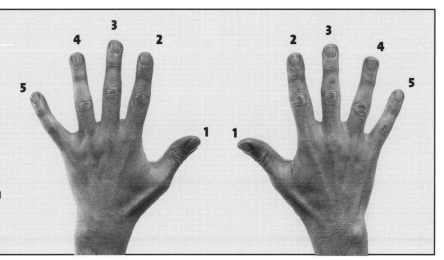

Activity

Placing your fingers on five consecutive white notes, play these finger patterns in different places on the piano. Listen to the contrasting pattern of sounds that these make and discuss them with your teacher. Decide which ones you like the best.

Count a steady pulse in "4" as you play.

L.H. 1 3 1 3 2 3 2 3 1 2 3 2 3 4 5 5   R.H. 1 2 1 2 3 2 3 2 3 4 5 4 3 2 1 1

Using this idea, make up some of your own patterns. Make a note of the ones you like most—you'll soon be composing like Beethoven!

Pieces for Lesson 1

Merrily We Roll Along

Traditional

Clap through the rhythm, counting aloud, before you play. Always play with a slight emphasis on the first pulse in every bar. This helps add shape and direction to the music.

Notice the patterns in the music. Some sections are repeated. What about the shapes in the music?

First Steps

Hayward

Follow the shapes and count a steady pulse before you play. Remember: you control the speed.

A Gentle Jog

Hayward

Set up both hands before playing and read the music in the order that it is written.

goals:

1. Legato
2. Rests

3. Repeat signs
4. Starting to coordinate the hands

Touch

There are many different ways to play the keys, and the sound that comes out from the piano will change accordingly. Linking the sounds smoothly together is the most frequently used touch and is called **legato playing**.

Imagine your fingers are walking along: at no point can both fingers be in the air together. Practice the movement on a hard surface first, and then transfer the movement to adjacent notes on the piano.

Listen very carefully to each new note and make sure that two sounds don't overlap or have a big gap between them.

Remember to play all exercises in both hands.

Never let one hand become more advanced than the other.

Exercise 1: Strolling

Hayward

Notice the double barline with dots at the end of this piece. This symbol is a *repeat sign*, and means that the piece should be played again from the beginning.

GOLDEN RULES

Keep your eyes looking ahead when reading and playing.

Listen closely to every note. Are they all legato?

Stay relaxed at all times. Check your shoulders, arms and hands.

Exercise 2:

Notice the shapes in the music and make sure you play these on the keyboard.

Aim for equal pressure and note-length throughout, and keep a steady pulse as you play.

Rests

When no music is being played, symbols are used to show silence.

whole-note rest   half-note rest   quarter-note rest

Using this chart, go back through each piece you have already played and with the help of your teacher fill in all the missing rests so that the music is complete.

Coordination

Now's the time to play with both hands together, before they learn too many separate tricks!

Tap your hands together on your lap. Make sure that they fall exactly together and in a steady pulse.

Now tap your right hand twice to every one tap in your left hand, and then swap hands.

This is a great way to start your two hands working together, but with some independence. Aim to do this for a few minutes every day—you'll soon get the hang of it.

Pieces for Lesson 2

Old MacDonald

Traditional

Watch out for the rests.

Watch out for the repeat signs here: the whole piece is played twice through.

Song Of The Volga Boatmen

Russian traditional

goals:

1. Repeated notes
2. Reading new music
3. Thirds
4. Dotted half notes
5. Tied notes
6. Whole note

READING NEW MUSIC

Make a habit of following the general shape of music and the intervals (distances) between the notes that make up each tune.
Keep your eyes moving ahead of your hands, counting steadily all the time.
Aim to read something new every time you play. This way, sight-reading will become much easier and your playing will become more fluent.

Exercise 1: Sight-reading

Notice any repeated patterns, and decide which fingers to start with.

Look at the range of notes used.

Exercise 2: Sight-reading

Count a steady pulse and read ahead as you play. Notice how the music doesn't always move stepwise from one note to the next. In this piece the intervals are mainly thirds—an important interval on the piano.

DOTTED HALF NOTES

A dot beside a note adds half the length of the note: 𝅗𝅥. = 𝅗𝅥 + ♩

Pieces for Lesson 3

Au Clair de la Lune

French traditional

The repeat sign at the end of the fourth bar tells you to play the first four bars again before continuing.

Notice the note in the fourth bar: this is a whole note and has a value of four quarter notes.

Repeated notes
can be tricky: make sure they are played steadily and evenly.

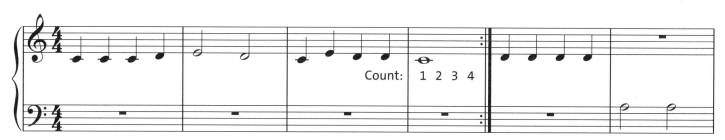

Twinkle Twinkle

Traditional

Pieces for Lesson 3

14–15

Row, Row, Row Your Boat
Traditional

Notice the new time signature: this piece has a count of three in each bar.

The rest symbol ▬ indicates a whole bar's rest. Also, take a look at the curved line joining the notes in bars 7 and 8. This is a **tie**. Ties join two notes together, creating a longer single note.

Count: 1   2   3   1   2   3   1   2   3

16–17

Camptown Races
Stephen Foster

Notice the dotted half notes in this piece: they always last for three beats.

1. **Eighth notes**
2. **New notes for the left hand**

3. **Playing hands together**
4. **Dynamics – loud and quiet**

Eighth notes

Eighth note and eighth-note rest

Eighth notes in pairs
(worth one quarter note per pair)

Eighth notes as a group
(worth one half note)

Practice playing and counting these rhythms, using different fingers and notes.

Play the hands separately and together, experimenting with different combinations of notes.

Count: 1   2   3   4   1   2 and 3   4   1 and 2 and 3   4   1 and 2   3   4

Exercise 1: New Bass Notes

Practice this exercise in your left hand, following the pattern of intervals carefully as you play.

C   E   G

Exercise 2: Pease Pudding

Count: 1   2 and 3 - 4   1   2 and 3 - 4   1   2 and 3 and 4 and   1   2 and 3 - 4

Exercise 3: Yankee Doodle

Lesson 4

Now hands together – a real treat!

First tap through the coordination exercise away from the piano. Do you remember this from lesson 2?

Dynamics

Notes and rhythms are two of the elements of music, but without expression, music can be lifeless and mechanical.

One of the obvious ways of introducing *color* into music is to play sections of pieces or phrases at different levels of loudness.

f stands for the word *forte* and means loud.   *p* stands for the word *piano* which means quiet.

Always listen closely as you change the sound, and avoid hitting the keys.

Pieces for Lesson 4

Old Woman   Folk Song

Are your shoulders relaxed? Review the section on posture (p. 7) if you are feeling tense or tired.

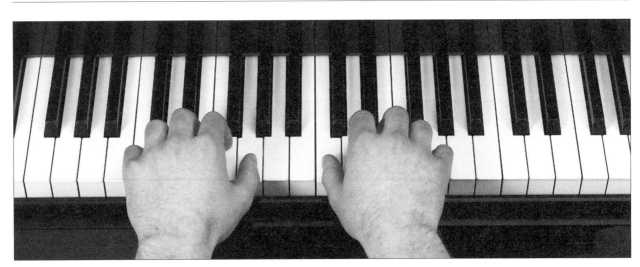

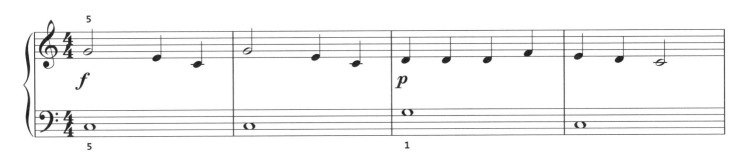

Pieces for Lesson 4

Ode To Joy

Beethoven

Frère Jacques

French traditional

Lesson 5 goals:

1. Building coordination skills   **2. Using dynamics creatively**

Coordination

The pieces in this lesson are designed to consolidate and improve your coordination skills.

Try the exercises below: count a steady pulse and set both hands up before playing each piece.

Coordination warm-ups nos. 1, 2 & 3

Repeat these exercises regularly until you are able to play them without hesitation.

Coordination is a key skill for pianists. Using both hands equally in a skilled activity is quite unusual. For this reason it's important to practice coordination with exercises like this from the outset.

Exercises 1 and 2:

Exercise 3:

DYNAMICS: YOU DECIDE!

Decide on some dynamics for the next two pieces,
and experiment until you are satisfied with the effect.

When you are happy with the sound, write the dynamics into the music.

Pieces for Lesson 5

Lightly Row

Traditional

If you are concentrating on the music, it's easy to forget about your posture and technique. Make sure you are relaxed, with a nice straight back, and that your hands aren't slumped on the keyboard.

Pieces for Lesson 5

London Bridge

Traditional

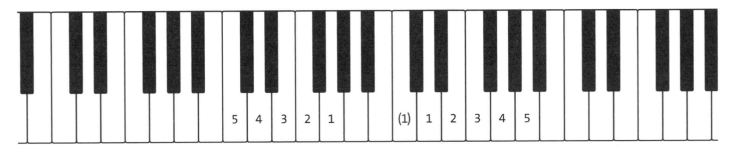

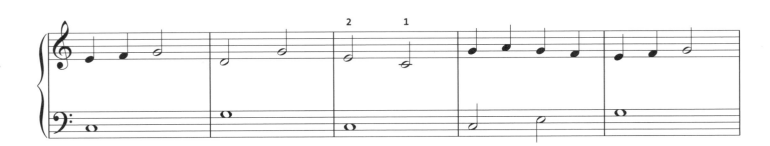

26•27 *Go Tell Aunt Nancy*

Traditional

Pieces for Lesson 5

Autumn (from *The Four Seasons*)

Vivaldi

Play the left hand through a few times to establish the rhythmic shape.

Skip To My Lou

Traditional

Stretch your thumb down in bar 3 to this new right-hand note, **B**.

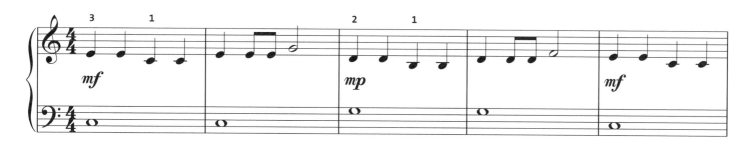

test: *for* Lessons 1 to 5

(10)

1. Note values and counts

Fill in the note values above the staff and the counts below the staff.

(10)

2. Rest values

Name the rests and say how many counts each is worth.

(10)

3. Note names

Name the notes:

(10)

4. Fingering

Decide on the fingering for this tune, then play it at sight.

(10)

5. Naming ceremony

Name all the signs marked with a *:

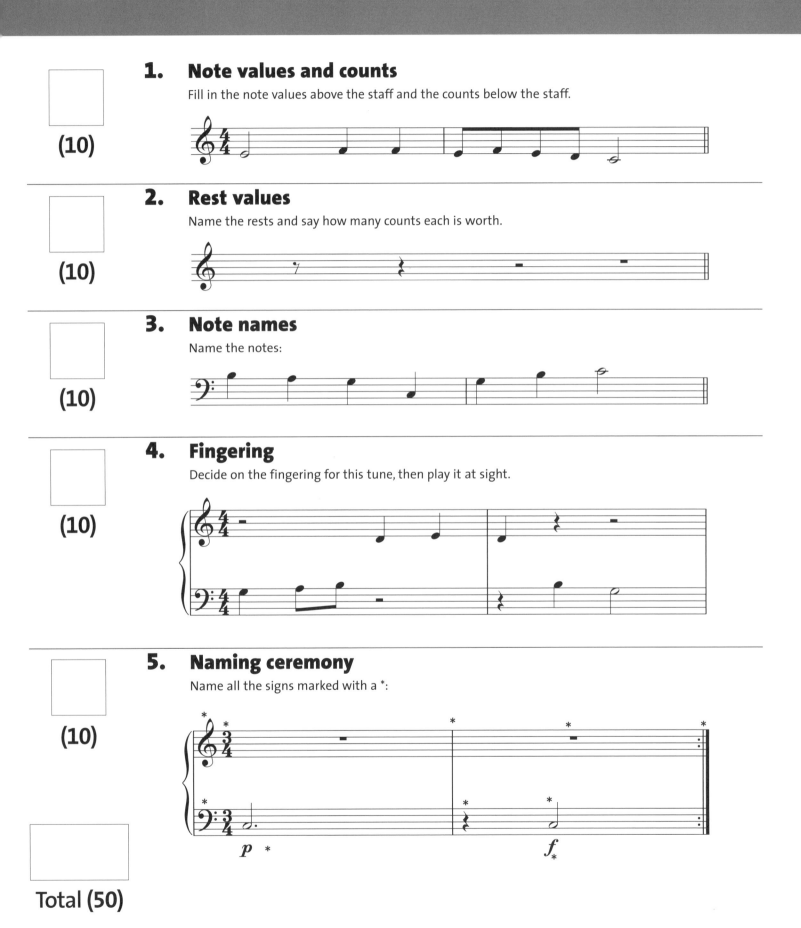

Total (50)

goals:

1. **Tones and semitones**
2. **Accidentals – sharps and flats**
3. **Dynamics –** *mf*
4. **Ostinato**

Tones and semitones

Intervals (the distance between notes of different pitches) are measured in **semitones**.

The *semitone*, the smallest interval on the keyboard, is the distance between any two neighboring keys. Try finding pairs of notes a semitone apart and listen to the sound they make when played together.

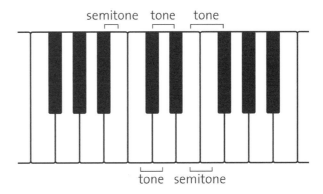

A **tone** is *twice* the distance of a semitone.
Notice that this can mean a mix of white and black keys, two black keys, or two white keys.
Try finding pairs of notes a tone apart and compare the sound of a tone with that of a semitone.

Exercise 1: Tone and semitone workout

You'll soon notice that although the interval between one white key and the next is a tone, there are two places—between E and F, and between B and C, where the interval is only a semitone.

In lesson 8 you will learn more about intervals and scales.

Using the black keys

Now that you have been introduced to the black keys, you can play them in your music.

Black keys are indicated by the use of sharp (♯) and flat (♭) signs.

Sharps (♯) raise the pitch of a note by one semitone, and flats (♭) lower the pitch of a note by one semitone.

DYNAMICS

mf is short for *mezzo forte* – meaning moderately loud.

34–35 *Myra's Wedding* Scottish traditional

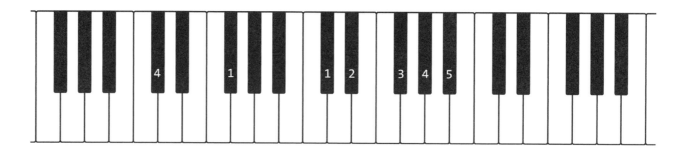

Notice that even if the same note is raised several times in one bar, it is only necessary to write the ♯ symbol once.

Improvise

In *March Slave* (opposite), you will notice that the left hand has a repeating phrase (*ostinato*).

Once you have played through the pieces in this lesson, try building your own ostinato using the same notes as the one in *March Slave*. Feel free to extend the pattern to more than one bar in length.

Finally, choose some different notes and make up an entirely new ostinato. What notes might you use for a melody to play above it?

Pieces for Lesson 6

Russian Lament
Hayward

You will need to move your fingers in towards the back of the keyboard to reach the black keys easily.

March Slave
Tchaikovsky

Notice that the bass clef pattern is repeated throughout this piece: this is known as an **ostinato** (or *riff*) and is a really useful tool for improvising.

36-37

Lesson 7 goals:

1. Shaping music – phrasing
2. More dynamics – *mp* and *pp*
3. Upbeats – anacrusis
4. Pause

Phrasing

Like language, music has punctuation to help add shape to what could otherwise be just strings of random sounds.

Playing *legato* is the first stage of using musical punctuation. A phrase mark illustrates a musical sentence, meaning that the notes are played legato and with subtle shaping. Think of inflection in speech.

Sing the tune through a few times in one breath to help feel the phrase.

Notice the rising bass part.

Play it through on its own a couple of times.

Exercise 1: Drink To Me Only With Thine Eyes

English traditional

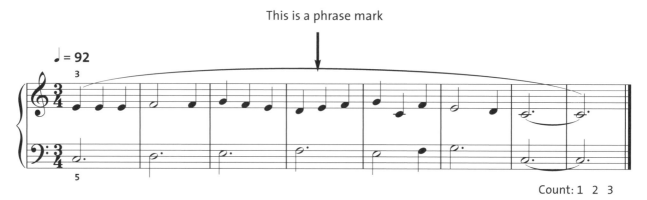

This is a phrase mark

Count: 1 2 3

DYNAMICS

mp *mezzo piano*, meaning moderately soft   *pp* *pianissimo*, meaning very softly

---

Exercise 2: Now The Day Is Over

Barnby

28

UPBEATS

Music doesn't always begin with a complete bar.

The remaining pieces in this lesson begin with a shorter bar (an *anacrusis*),
which is balanced by another shorter bar at the end of the piece.
These two bars together add up to one complete bar.

Where the anacrusis is worth a single beat, this is known as an **upbeat**.

Anacrusis warm-ups

Exercise 3: Cockles And Mussels
Irish traditional

Notice the interval that begins this piece and the fingering needed.

Count: 1 2 3

Exercise 4: Oh When The Saints Go Marching In
Spiritual

Count: and 4 and   1   2   3 and 4 and

How is your posture?

Check your back, shoulders, arms, wrists and fingers.

Is your seat set at a comfortable height?

Pieces for Lesson 7

For He's A Jolly Good Fellow

Traditional

Notice the sign ⌢ in bar 12 that looks a little like an eye. This sign is called a **pause** (or *fermata*).
When this sign appears, the note should be held for longer than usual.

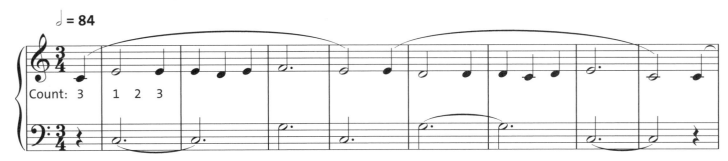

Now decide on some dynamics to help create the right mood for this piece.

Oh When The Saints Go Marching In

Traditional

Compare this piece with the previous version: now the first three notes are played as quarter notes and all the note values are twice as long. This piece includes a large number of rests, so keep counting as you play.

goals:

1. **Thumb turns**
2. **Introducing scales and keys**
3. **Make a tune**

Using the thumb

So far, most of the pieces played use no more than a five-note range—convenient for the number of fingers on each hand!

However, the piano has many more notes, and by turning the thumb under the hand or turning fingers over the thumb, the whole keyboard becomes accessible.

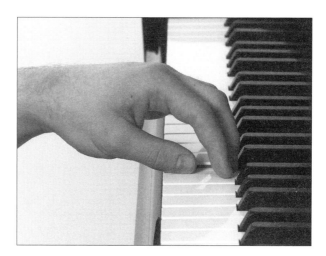

In this lesson you will explore the major scale.

Scales are an important part of piano technique, and it is essential to use the correct fingering.

Aim for a fluid, controlled movement.

Preliminary exercises

Practice these every time you play to help develop natural and relaxed thumb turns.

Begin on C each time. Practice equally with each hand and do not swing the elbow out. Make the thumb do the work.

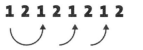  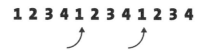

The major scale

The notes of the major scale follow a particular pattern of intervals.

Most of the notes are a tone apart, but between the 3rd and 4th notes of the scale, and again between the 7th and 8th notes of the scale, the interval is only half as much: a semitone.

Tone	Tone	Semitone	Tone	Tone	Tone	Semitone

1   2   3   4   5   6   7   8

Play from C to C using only the white keys, and notice the interval at each step.

You will see that the pattern of intervals follows the diagram above. Memorize **T T S T T T S**.

Now begin on any note and work out the same pattern of intervals. You will soon see that depending on which note you begin, you will need a different number of sharps or flats to keep the **T T S T T T S** sequence going.

Lesson 8

Exercise 1: C major scale

| R.H. | 1 | 2 | 3 | 1 | 2 | 3 | 4 | 5 |
| L.H. | 5 | 4 | 3 | 2 | 1 | 3 | 2 | 1 |

Play with a steady pulse and a sense of direction.

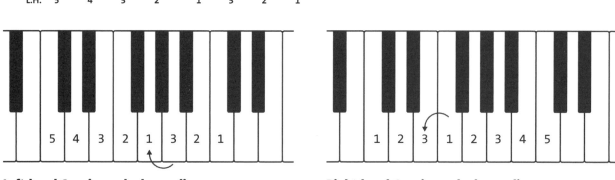

Left-hand C major scale descending   **Right-hand C major scale descending**

Exercise 2: G major scale

The G major scale includes new notes—but you can use the fingering shape shown above to play this scale.

For the G major scale, you'll need to play F♯, shown by the ♯ symbol at the beginning of the piece. This is known as the key signature.

| R.H. | 1 | 2 | 3 | 1 | 2 | 3 | 4 | 5 |
| L.H. | 5 | 4 | 3 | 2 | 1 | 3 | 2 | 1 |

SCALES

Scales are great fun to play.
They build good finger action and form the basis of musical awareness.

Try the following variations so your scale practice remains fresh:

• Play them smoothly, slowly and quietly

• Play them fast and loudly, or fast and quietly

• Play them very softly

• Emphasize every other note to give a lilting feel

There are lots of different ways to play scales. Find a different way every day.

Pieces for Lesson 8

Westminster Chimes

Crotch

Following the diagrams opposite, be sure to keep the fingers moving in the correct sequence.

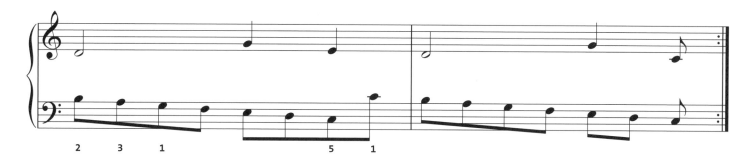

Remember to count the upbeat carefully.

Twist And Turn

Hayward

46–47

The new sign ——————— in bar 4 is a **crescendo** mark. *Crescendo* means grow gradually louder.

At the end of bar 2, stretch out the right hand to reach the next note, B, with finger 3.

In the final few bars, work out the best fingering for yourself.

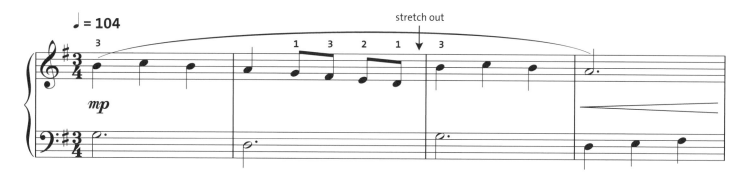

Pieces for Lesson 8

Country Gardens

Traditional

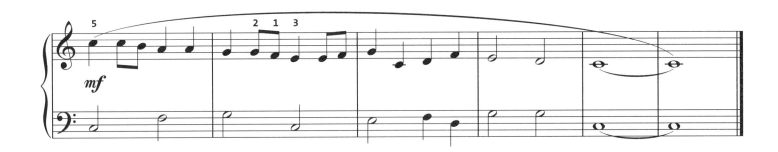

Make a tune

Using the first five notes of the G major scale, make up four bar-tunes in $\frac{4}{4}$ in the right hand.

Begin and end on G and aim to use a mixture of quarter notes, eighth notes and half notes.

Make up a different one every time you practice. Write down your favorite one.

You could also try adding an *ostinato*.

goals:

1. Dotted rhythms
2. Minor keys

Dotted rhythms

A dot to the right of a note increases its value by half.

A half note with a dot lasts for three beats, and a quarter note with a dot is worth one and a half beats.

Exercise 1:

The tie, used up until now to join notes from one bar to another, can also be used within a bar.

The first quarter note and eighth note of bars three and four in this piece are joined to make a note worth one and a half beats: more simply written as a dotted quarter note.

Dotted quarter notes are often coupled with a single eighth note to give a long-short rhythm.

Try the following exercise to hear how this rhythm sounds.

Exercise 2:

Count: 1 2 and 3 4 1 2 and 3 4 1 2 and 3 4 and 1 2 and 3 4

Play this exercise in the left hand too— and, once you've looked at the section on minor scales below, work out what key it's in and try it in E minor as well.

50 51

Exercise 3: All Through The Night

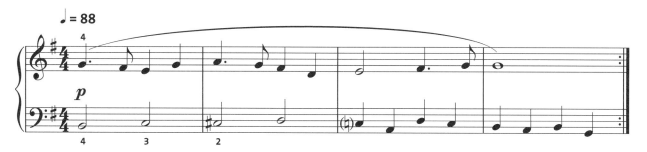

Largo (from *the New World Symphony*)   Dvořák

♩ = 80

Count: 1   2 and 3   4

Minor scales

Melodies built using notes of the major scale often have a bright, bold character.

Another common scale from which to choose notes for a melody is the minor scale.

The mood of a piece in a minor key can be quite somber.

Play from A to A using only the white notes and check the distances between each note.

Compare the sequence of intervals with that of a major scale. You will notice that the semitones now occur between the 2nd and 3rd notes, and again between the 5th and 6th notes.

Tone	Tone	Semitone	Tone	Tone	Tone	Semitone
1	2	3	4	5	6	7 8

A minor uses the same notes as C major, and E minor uses the same notes as G major. They are said to be *relatives*: A minor is the relative minor of C major, and E minor is the relative minor of G major.

Listen closely to the character of the scale compared to that of C major.

Let's have a look at the minor scale beginning on A and E. In lesson 15, you will discover other minor scales. The ones used here are known as *natural* minor.

A minor scale

Using the same fingering as for C major, be sure to try both scales here with each hand.

5 4 3 2 1 3 2 1

E minor scale

1 2 3 1 2 3 4 5

Watch your finger, hand and arm positions, and play with a steady pulse.

Rit: short for *ritenuto* = get a little slower

The long hairpin ➤ means *diminuendo* = get gradually softer.

Pieces for Lesson 9

Greensleeves *(adapted)*   Traditional

You will need to lift your right hand in bar 8 and reposition it for the correct fingering.

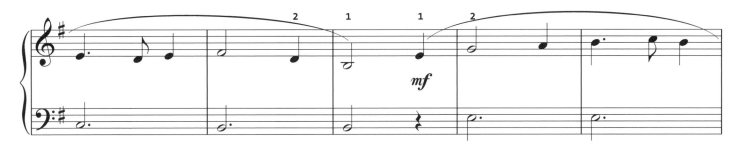

Sonata *(adapted)*   Mozart

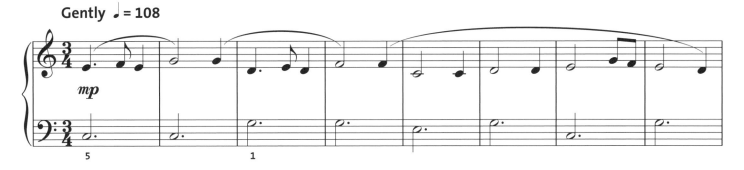

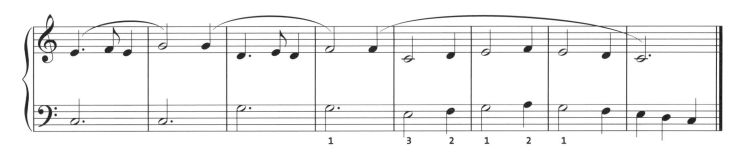

1. Left-hand work
2. Dynamics: *ff*

3. Common time
4. First and second endings

Use of the left hand

The left hand is often responsible for accompanying a melody, adding harmony to a tune. Practice the following exercises to help build up dexterity and control of the hand.

Exercise 1:

Play this shape in each of the keys played to date. Note the differences in sound type from major to minor.

Stay relaxed as you play, following the shape of the notes with an easy wrist movement.

Exercise 2:

Write in the best fingering for this bass line.

Aim to play evenly and with a sense of energy.

Exercise 3:

The next exercise combines two notes together.

This is the basis of blocks of sound known as chords: more about this in lesson 11.

Notice that G is common to each interval. Listen to the effect of combining notes together.

Try these exercises at various dynamics, right up to *ff*.

DYNAMICS

ff meaning fortissimo = very loud

Common time

The $\frac{4}{4}$ time signature is often referred to as *common time*, and can be written like this: **C**.

First and second endings

In the following pieces, play the repeated section as usual.

On the second time through, skip the music under the "first ending" and play the "second ending" instead.

Pieces for Lesson 10

Jingle Bells

Traditional

We Three Kings

Traditional

Take a close look at the right-hand fingering from bar 6 onward.

Pieces for Lesson 10

 62–63

Away In A Manger

Traditional

The diagonal line at the first bar indicates that the tune begins in the bass clef but then moves straight into the treble.

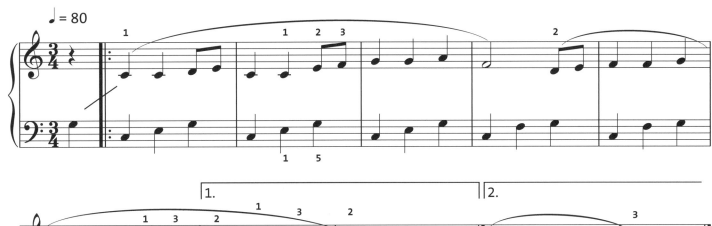

64–65

Good King Wenceslas

Traditional

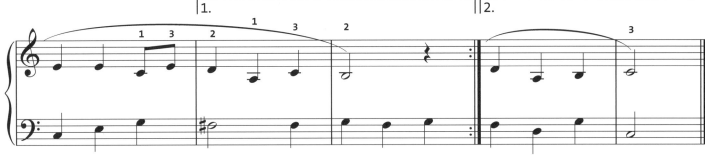

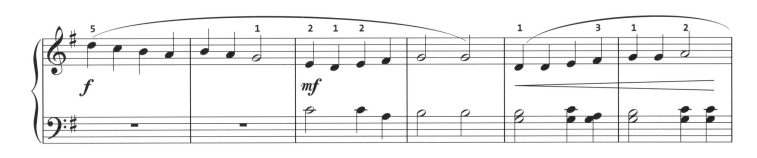

1. Intervals

Write the letter **T** or **S** between the notes to indicate which intervals are tones and which are semitones:

(10)

2. Name and play

Name and then play each note:

(12)

3. Counting

Write the correct count at each notehead:

(8)

4. Scale exercise

Write the first five notes of the minor scale to which this key signature belongs:

(10)

5. Naming ceremony

Name all the signs marked with a *, and give the correct key:

(10)

Total **(50)**

1. Chords
2. Arpeggios

Chords

The word "chord" literally means "sounding two or more notes together. "

Many different note combinations are possible, but for now we will work with one of the most common types: the *triad*. Triads are made using particular notes from a scale.

Notice the pattern that appears on the music when triads are written down.

Remember to practice equally with both hands— and close your eyes as you play to increase your confidence and awareness.

F triad in the left hand

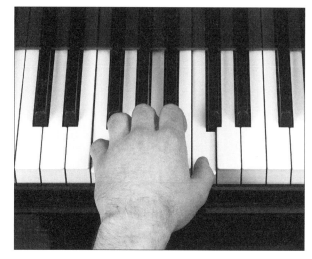

C triad in the right hand

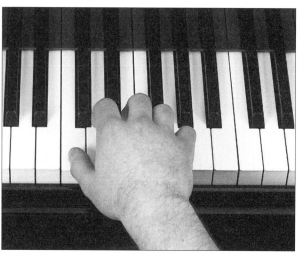

Try building triads starting on each different note of a scale and listen to the different sounds. Some will be major, others will be minor—and some will be neither!

Roman numerals are used to label the different steps of a scale: look at the diagram below.

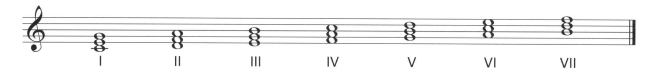

I   II   III   IV   V   VI   VII

The use of triads in the left hand is an important way to provide an accompaniment for a right-hand melody—although triads can also be played in the right hand, of course.

Chords I, IV and V are the most commonly used chords in each scale.

Exercise 1:

Work out which chord is which in these warm-up routines.

Play this exercise until you can do it without looking down at the keyboard.

Exercise 2:

Arpeggios

Arpeggios are another way of presenting chord shapes within a scale.

This time, instead of playing the notes together, they are played in sequence.

Take the 1st, 3rd, 5th, and *octave* note of any scale to build an arpeggio.

Finding the notes that make an arpeggio

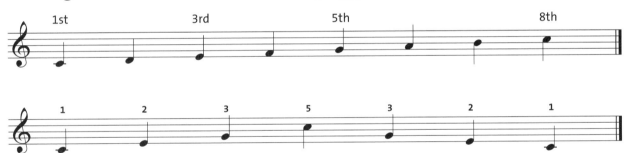

Play this arpeggio in C major from the music and then work out the arpeggios in all the other scales used so far.

Say the notes as you play them: as you start to memorize the patterns your chord knowledge will improve.

C H O R D S

Chords are such an important and common part of music that in rock, pop and jazz, chord symbols are often used rather than writing out all the notes in full.

You'll see symbols such as **C7**, **Dm6**, and **Fmaj7**, which will give you an idea of the notes involved, but the exact timing and order will be up to you.

A good knowledge of chords is essential for the pianist or keyboard player in these styles. Take a look at the pull-out included with this book for some common chords, and experiment with different voicings (the exact placing of the notes on the keyboard).

Pieces for Lesson 11

Piece With No Name

Hayward

Name the chords in this piece and add some expression marks. Then think of a title to suit the mood.

Amazing Grace

Traditional

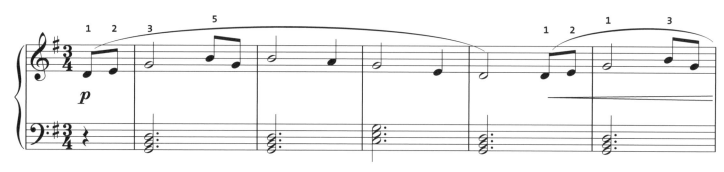

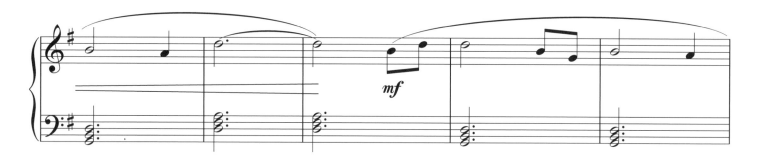

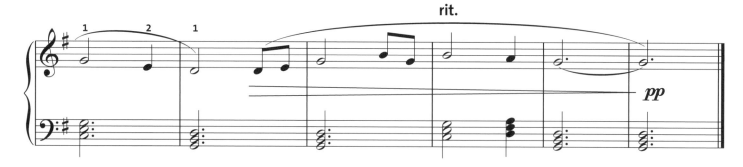

Pentatonic scales

So far, you have used traditional types of scales (keys)—major and minor—typical in Western classical music.

However, much traditional music uses the *pentatonic* scale. The "blues" in particular uses a version of this. See how the scales below are based on scales you have learned, but with certain notes "missing."

C pentatonic

As the name suggests, a pentatonic scale has five notes. The blues makes extensive use of this scale.

A minor pentatonic

Work out the pentatonic scales based on G major and E minor—then write them down.

G major

E minor

Chords

Chords offer a wealth of opportunities for a pianist and are used to create a wide range of effects, often in accompaniment. Try the examples below:

Exercise 1: Drone Bass

The tiny note at the beginning of each chord should be played as quickly as possible.
It is known as an *acciaccatura*. Here, it should help the drone to sound a little like bagpipes.

Play all three notes together and immediately lift the acciaccatura, leaving the whole notes to play on.

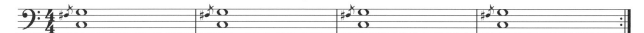

Exercise 2: Waltz Bass

Notice how the chords I, IV and V are used in this piece: the notes are not always in the order in which they appear in a triad. This is known as an *inversion*.

This left-hand exercise should sound like the famous "oom-pa-pa" of a brass band. Make the 2nd and 3rd beats nice and light.

Exercise 3: Broken-up Chords

This pattern is known as *Alberti* bass. When you are able to play this exercise fluently, try using the chords from exercise 2 to create a new *Alberti* bass line.

Improvisation

Using the combination of a drone bass and pentatonic scale of your choice, create a melody with a Scottish feel in eight bars of $\frac{4}{4}$ time.

Pieces for Lesson 12

Myra's Wedding   Scottish traditional

With energy

Now for fun, play this whole piece a semitone lower in F♯ major!

Pieces for Lesson 12

Tales Of Hoffmann

With a gentle sway

Can Can

Notice the interval in the first ending, right hand: an octave. This is a very important interval for pianists to know and play. Add your own dynamics to bring this piece to life.

With drive

Lesson 13

goals:

1. New keys – F major and D minor
2. New touch – staccato
3. Naturals

Keys with flats

Major scales either raise (with a ♯) or lower (with a ♭) notes to keep the **T T S T T T S** sequence intact.

F major requires a flat at the fourth step of the scale to create a semitone between the 3rd and 4th notes.

Exercise 1:

Notice the different fingering needed to play F major in the right hand.

This is one of the irregular scale finger patterns to remember.

F major

| | R.H | 1 | 2 | 3 | 4 | 1 | 2 | 3 | 4 | 3 | 2 | 1 | 4 | 3 | 2 | 1 |
| | L.H. | 5 | 4 | 3 | 2 | 1 | 3 | 2 | 1 | 2 | 3 | 1 | 2 | 3 | 4 | 5 |

The fingering for D minor is the same as for A minor and E minor.

D minor

Try to recall the fingering patterns used previously to play this new scale.

Play both scales through with both hands separately—sing as you play.

Work out chords I, IV and V from F major and arpeggios from both scales and make a note of them below:

Staccato

Staccato (meaning detached) is a short, clipped note made by releasing keys quickly. It produces the opposite effect to legato and creates a great contrast. Staccato notes look like this:

First bounce wrists up and down away from the keyboard to get a good basic action. Then, keeping the same movement, play up and down the first five notes of both F major and D minor.

Listen closely to the sound of notes played staccato and close your eyes so that you "feel" the movement of good staccatos—they need to be controlled and consistent.

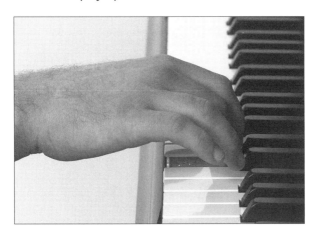

48

Pieces for Lesson 13

Andante (from *Surprise Symphony*)

Haydn

The small hairpin symbols ➤ on the half notes in these pieces are *accents*.

These notes require more weight than usual.

This Old Man

Traditional

Work out the best fingering for this piece before you play it through.

Notice how this piece—and many others—is made up of scale and arpeggio fragments

Pieces for Lesson 13

82–83

Scarborough Fair

Traditional

Notice the natural symbol (♮) in bar 9 in the right hand.

The natural cancels a symbol in the key signature, in this case the B♭, so here you are asked to play a B.

Slow and thoughtful

goals:

1. **Slurs**
2. **Basic blues**
3. **Swing eighth notes**

Slurs

Slurring (moving smoothly from one note to another with clear shaping) is an important technique for pianists. It is possible to have three- or four-note slurs, and the approach is the same. However, the two-note slur needs to be mastered first.

When slurring, the first of the two notes needs a slight sense of weight, while the second needs to be slightly quieter, tapering off in tone and time.

Try thinking of **weight** (on the first note) and **float** (on the second note) while playing these warm-up exercises. Remember to involve both hands and all fingers to achieve a balance of technical ability.

Exercise 1:

Play this exercise a number of times, changing the fingering each time until all combinations have been used.

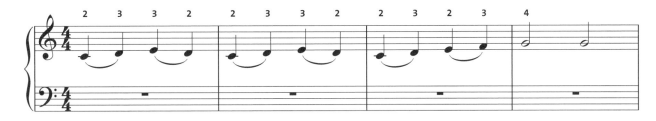

Using the same musical shape, play this exercise in both G and F major. Playing the same shape in different keys is called transposing music.

Basic blues and swing time

A relative of jazz, the *blues* has its roots in the music of twentieth-century African-American folk music.

It describes a state of mind—feeling blue—as well as the chord progressions used as a basis of the style, most often twelve bars in length. Melodies over this progression commonly use a minor pentatonic scale, but with the addition of a "blue note," i.e., the flatted 5th note of the given key.

Notice how the 3rd and 7th, also flatted when compared with the major scale, have a very bluesy feel.

Exercise 2: Blues scale in C

Play this blues scale, listening closely to the sound. When you have it under your fingers, sing along as you play.

Exercise 3: Twelve-bar blues chord progression

The chords in this exercise are I, IV and V in the key of C, but here they have been written out using their letter names, as is common in jazz and blues.

Once you have memorized the chord progression, practice playing the riff below in the left hand as you play notes from the blues scale in the right hand: listen to the way it all fits together.

Once you feel confident, try playing this chord sequence with your eyes closed, sensing when the chord is about to change.

♩ = 96

Exercise 4: Blues riff

Here is a *riff*, or short repeated phrase, that works well for the C chord.

Now work out a version for the F and G chords and play through the complete twelve-bar sequence.

Here, the middle note of the C chord has been left out, and an extra note has been added on the 3rd and 4th beats of the bar. The added note, A, is the 6th note counting up from C.

This makes this a C6 chord, a very common sound for the blues.

Swing

In classical music all eighth notes are played exactly as written: that is, lasting half as long as a quarter note.

In jazz and blues, however, eighth notes are normally played unevenly, with the first of each pair longer than half a beat, and the second shorter to compensate. This is called *swing*.

Remember not to play the eighth notes too "straight," but instead give them a healthy bounce.

You might imagine the beat divided into three, with the first two-thirds for the first eighth note and the final third for the second eighth note.

Play any scale with which you feel confident, but instead of playing it with a steady pulse in which all the eighth notes are the same length, try playing them with a swing feel.

As you get used to the feel of swing, you can try applying it to other pieces you've learned—with some surprising results!

Pieces for Lesson 14

Ploddin' Round The Ranch

Hayward

86–87

Slow swing ♩ = 80

The left-hand eighth notes are played with a swing feel in this piece: make sure you create a good swaying feel.

Skater's Waltz

Waldteufel

88–89

Gently ♩ = 120

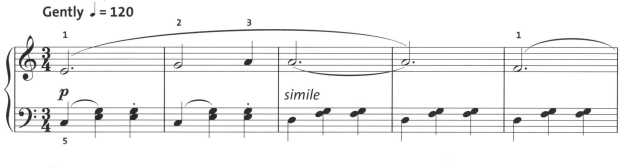

No swing here, but graceful, balanced slurs.

Simile means continue in the same way throughout.

goals:

1. The changing minor scale
2. Consolidating skills
3. Improvising the blues

The changing minor scale

Unlike the major scale, the minor scale can be presented in a number of ways.

The minor scale studied in lesson 9 used exactly the same notes as its relative major.
Listen to that minor scale again, and notice how the last interval of the scale, being a tone, is not as "final" as the last semitone of a major scale. Raising the 7th note of a minor scale gives the top note more of a sense of arrival, and is very useful for building chords—hence the name *harmonic* minor.

Exercise 1:

Notice how the alterations to these scales are included within the notes rather than in the key signature: these are known as *accidentals*.

Play through carefully, singing as you go, and listen to the character of the scale.

A harmonic minor

The interval between the 6th and 7th notes of the harmonic minor scale sounds rather awkward, and not very useful for building melodies. So a further adjustment, a raised 6th, is necessary to make the scale more tuneful:

Exercise 2:

Note that the 6th and 7th are only raised on the way up. This is so that the scale still retains its "minor" quality on the way down.

A melodic minor

Now work out the new (harmonic and melodic) versions of the E and D minor scales.

Improvising the blues

Using the riff from *Sad And Blue* (page 56), improvise a new melody in the right hand.

You need only put one note in a bar if you wish, but remember which chord is being used and choose a note that belongs to it so that the tune "fits."

With each new improvisation, aim to use a few more notes, including some "blue notes" (flat 3rd, flat 5th and flat 7th) to draw out the style of the music.

Pieces for Lesson 15

Hava Nagila

Israeli traditional

Begin very slowly and use accelarando throughout.

The tempo, or speed, of this piece changes as it progresses—from a ponderous, deliberately slow tempo, accelerating to a frantic finish!

Try to make the accelarando (acceleration) constant, and make sure you don't get too fast too soon.

TEMPO TERMS

Italian terms are often used to show the tempo of a piece of music.
Here are a few of the most common terms, in order of speed:

Largo very slow   **Andante** at a walking pace   **Allegro** fast
Adagio slow   **Moderato** moderately   **Presto** very fast

Pieces for Lesson 15

90–91   *Lullaby*   Brahms

Listen to the balance between the right-hand melody and left-hand accompaniment. Aim for a light left hand.

Gently rocking

92–93   *Sad And Blue*   Hayward

The wiggly line at the end means to roll the chord by playing from the lowest to the highest notes, holding each down as you go, until there is a block of sound. Experiment with different combinations for this chord.

With a slow swing ♩ = 69

Pieces for Lesson 15

Skye Boat Song

Scottish traditional

Listen closely to bar 11. What do you notice?

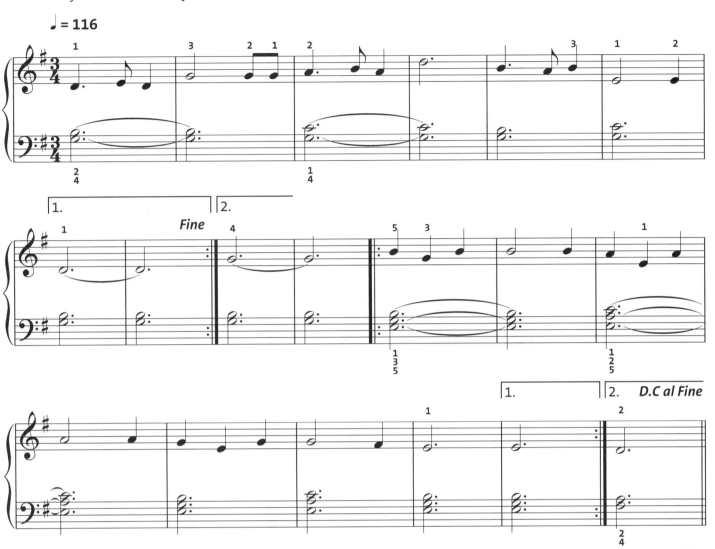

Little Sonata

C. H. Wilton

Pieces for Lesson 15

Quadrille

Haydn

A Song For Olive

Hayward

Moderato

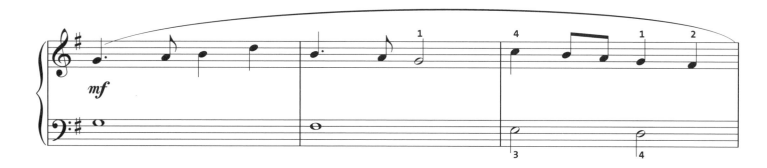

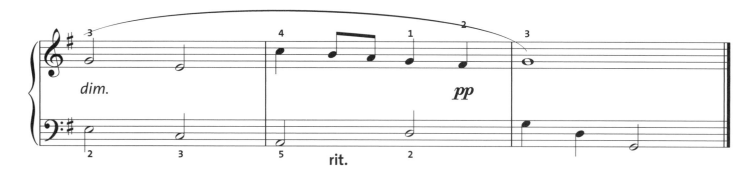

1. Keys and chords

Identify the key of the piece, and—using both letters and Roman numerals—name the chords:

(10)

2. Arpeggios

Write the arpeggio of D minor and give the fingering for both hands:

(10)

3. Name and play

Name and play this scale:

(8)

4. Name and play

Name and play this scale:

(8)

5. Left-hand technique

By what name is this bass line known?

(4)

6. Naming ceremony

Name all the signs marked with a *, and write suitable fingering:

(10)

Total **(50)**

59

Performance Pieces

Fond Memories

Hayward

Slow and thoughtful

Performance Pieces

Walkin' The Walk

Hayward

Medium Rock

Performance Pieces

Minor Yours!

Hayward

Lento

Performance Pieces

On Top Of Old Smokey

Traditional

With a good swing

CD track listing

1. Virtuoso Performance: Minute Waltz (Chopin)
2. Merrily We Roll Along *demonstration*
3. Merrily We Roll Along *backing only*
4. First Steps *demonstration*
5. First Steps *backing only*
6. A Gentle Jog *demonstration*
7. A Gentle Jog *backing only*
8. Old MacDonald *demonstration*
9. Old MacDonald *backing only*
10. Song Of The Volga Boatmen *demonstration*
11. Song Of The Volga Boatmen *backing only*
12. Twinkle Twinkle *demonstration*
13. Twinkle Twinkle *backing only*
14. Row, Row, Row Your Boat *demonstration*
15. Row, Row, Row Your Boat *backing only*
16. Camptown Races *demonstration*
17. Camptown Races *backing only*
18. New Bass Notes *demonstration*
19. New Bass Notes *backing only*
20. Pease Pudding *demonstration*
21. Pease Pudding *backing only*
22. Yankee Doodle *demonstration*
23. Yankee Doodle *backing only*
24. Frère Jacques *demonstration*
25. Frère Jacques *backing only*
26. Go Tell Aunt Nancy *demonstration*
27. Go Tell Aunt Nancy *backing only*
28. Autumn, *from* Four Seasons *demonstration*
29. Autumn, *from* Four Seasons *backing only*
30. Skip To My Lou *demonstration*
31. Skip To My Lou *backing only*
32. Tone And Semitone Workout *demonstration*
33. Tone And Semitone Workout *backing only*

34. Myra's Wedding *demonstration*
35. Myra's Wedding *backing only*
36. March Slave *demonstration*
37. March Slave *backing only*
38. Drink To Me Only With Thine Eyes *demonstration*
39. Drink To Me Only With Thine Eyes *backing only*
40. Now The Day Is Over *demonstration*
41. Now The Day Is Over *backing only*
42. For He's A Jolly Good Fellow *demonstration*
43. For He's A Jolly Good Fellow *backing only*
44. When The Saints Go Marching In *demonstration*
45. When The Saints Go Marching In *backing only*
46. Twist And Turn *demonstration*
47. Twist And Turn *backing only*
48. Country Gardens *demonstration*
49. Country Gardens *backing only*
50. All Through The Night *demonstration*
51. All Through The Night *backing only*
52. Largo, *from the* New World Symphony *demonstration*
53. Largo, *from the* New World Symphony *backing only*
54. Greensleeves *demonstration*
55. Greensleeves *backing only*
56. Sonata *demonstration*
57. Sonata *backing only*
58. Jingle Bells *demonstration*
59. Jingle Bells *backing only*
60. We Three Kings *demonstration*
61. We Three Kings *backing only*
62. Away In A Manger *demonstration*
63. Away In A Manger *backing only*
64. Good King Wenceslas *demonstration*
65. Good King Wenceslas *backing only*
66. Chord Warm-Up 1 *demonstration*
67. Chord Warm-Up 1 *backing only*
68. Chord Warm-Up 2 *demonstration*

69. Chord Warm-Up 2 *backing only*
70. Piece With No Name *demonstration*
71. Piece With No Name *backing only*
72. Amazing Grace *demonstration*
73. Amazing Grace *backing only*
74. Waltz Bass *demonstration*
75. Waltz Bass *backing only*
76. Tales Of Hoffmann *demonstration*
77. Tales Of Hoffmann *backing only*
78. Can Can *demonstration*
79. Can Can *backing only*
80. Andante, *from* Surprise Symphony *demonstration*
81. Andante, *from* Surprise Symphony *backing only*
82. Scarborough Fair *demonstration*
83. Scarborough Fair *backing only*
84. Twelve-Bar Blues *demonstration*
85. Twelve-Bar Blues *backing only*
86. Ploddin' Round The Ranch *demonstration*
87. Ploddin' Round The Ranch *backing only*
88. Skater's Waltz *demonstration*
89. Skater's Waltz *backing only*
90. Lullaby *demonstration*
91. Lullaby *backing only*
92. Sad And Blue *demonstration*
93. Sad And Blue *backing only*
94. Skye Boat Song *demonstration*
95. Skye Boat Song *backing only*
96. Little Sonata *demonstration*
97. Little Sonata *backing only*

How to use the CD

After track 1, which gives an idea of how the piano can sound, the tracks are listed in the order in which they appear in the book. Look for the ⊙ symbol in the book for the relevant demonstration or backing track.

1 2 3 4 5 6 7 8 9